# The Forked Rivers

# THE
# FORKED
# RIVERS

*Nancy Donegan*

Alice James Books
Cambridge, Massachusetts
1989

Copyright © 1989 by Nancy Donegan    All rights reserved.
Library of Congress Cataloging-In-Publication Data
Donegan, Nancy
I. *The Forked Rivers*
PS3554.046924F67   1989
811'.54 – dc 20        89-35793
                              CIP
ISBN    0-914086-89-8    paper

Illustration, cover and book design by Anna M. Pulaski
Cover Photography courtesy of Maureen O'Connell Palmer
Typeset by The Writer's Center, Bethesda, Maryland
First Printing by Malloy Lithographing, Ann Arbor, Michigan

ACKNOWLEDGEMENTS    The author wishes to thank the editors of the following publications
in which some of these poems, or earlier versions of them, first appeared: *Tendril, Bridgewater Arts,
Sounding/East, Dark Horse, Brown Journal of the Arts, Writ, Willow Springs.*

The publication of this book was made possible with support from the Massachusetts Council on the
Arts and Humanities, a state agency whose funds are recommended by the Governor and appropriated
by the State Legislature.

The author makes grateful acknowledgements to the Brockton Arts Lottery Commission for its
generous grant.

*Alice James Books are published by
the Alice James Poetry Cooperative, Inc.*

Alice James Books
33 Richdale Avenue
Cambridge, MA 02140

*For my mother Gertrude Crowe Warner
and my father Joseph A. Warner*

# Table of Contents

## P.S. for August

The cat left the carcass
of a rabbit on the porch
early this morning.
Its bloodless hind-paws
rigid as waxed leaves.

Forget-me-nots still glint
bright blue at the ledge.
Once I stencilled the borders
of our room, stippled paint
until my knuckles bled—
the color of your eyes impossible
to replicate.

Through the overhang of chokecherry
a spider's wire down.

We don't talk anymore.

I won't forget the sound
of a rabbit's light bones
sliding from my trowel,
a quenched field,
wordless ends.

# Vanishing Point

Once we watched a magician, tissue silk scarves
    of white and fuchsia
streaming from his sleeves, transmuted mid-air
    to doves and birds of paradise,
and we groaned for the one who soared to the spotlight
    blinded, tapping beyond reach.

The way you are disappearing is not theatrical. I knew
    you were a magician, your tongue
on my breasts and between my thighs was silk
    and my fingers' flutter on the bones
of your spine, wingbeats. That was illusion.

I am learning how silk may become anything in the mind
    and for no apparent reason
any creature may reel into a place at once luminous
    and totally obscure.

On the road to Wellfleet tonight miles of starlings
    line the telephone wires. The last one
lifts, flows on a current to the roosting trees, unaware
    of a watcher who counts the variable beats
required to reach a vanishing point, like listening
    for a coda, or the last note.

# The Forked Rivers

I His people have always lived in the cold place.
Albinos are common among them, and snow-blindness.
The ice is exceedingly deep. He despises machinery—
the logic of parts. A jack-hammer which might bore
to the bottom of the river rots in his shed. Still
there are shimmerings down in that muck, and legends
of rare jewels buried before the ice came.
Night after night his skate blades sing over the
surface. Their music is his heart's delight, dear
as his dream of immortality, the heavy old hemlocks
at the edge. As he circles, a few small figures
wave from the distance. Occasionally something
beneath him glistens. The moon spills its milk
over ice that holds like amnesia. No one
ever mentions the sea.


II You and I are luckier than the dead
who cannot lift a shovel
against the snow,
or hone an ax
to shatter the stubborn ice.


III The French riot against the Algerians
who stink from the work
they do for the Nationals
who would not labor
in such menial filth.
It is winter.
In spring someone
must clean the blinds.

IV    A man and a woman coexist,
sentries pacing a common zone.
A Cold War—
two people holding out
fistsfuls of snow.

V    And these are some myths that lasted:
poverty, chastity, obedience.

VI    Freeze frame:
their march across the Bering Strait
may have taken 25,000 years.
Cliffs of rotting ice at the borders,
white land beyond
thick as mountains.
Fire, their tender mercy.

VII    Snow is falling on the bronze statue
of Mary Dyer near Boston Common.
It seals her eyes and mouth. Dissenter,
Quaker, dervish, Winthrop's winterbane.
In 1660, Rev. John Wilson
offered his white linen handkerchief
to spare her the sight
of her hangman's noose.
She thanked him,
passed it back
folded in his hands.

VIII     Mother of Lies,
        the wind is my counsel.
        This is a prayer
        not that the dark will go
        but that we may see through it.

IX      There are towns in this county called Last Chance,
        Forked River, End of the Line. People attend
        town meeting religiously. They know every inch
        of their land, each penny in the local budget.
        The front pages of the newspapers print mostly
        news of tax increases, fires, Lion's Club,
        trash collection; in the back section Lebanon
        and slaughter, U.N. reports of famine from
        Kenya. This morning a woman named Carla wraps
        her garbage in yesterday's *Bulletin*. She
        falls on the icy steps and the paper scatters
        over the snow. Breathless, she sees photos,
        headlines. Her eyes sting—
        they are too close.

# Terminus

The force of the cold is in
its ubiquity. It is bonded
into his body, it urges frost
throughout his spirit. If the spirit
has eyes they are blinded and if those eyes
have learned anything, they are grateful
to be blind. But the eyes of his body
are fixed on instruments that probe
and chip at the thickening cells
which have already vaulted
into a white, faultless space beyond him.
How hotly he craves to breathe
even in this
neck-locked wrist-heavy mouth-stopping
winter that is all at once everywhere
he has been or can be.

## What She Can See Here

Tulips show you
how to be shining outside,
oozing calm,
each with its cheerful crown
of yellow, red.

Smooth out your hair,
the mirror returns what is given
and the tulips appear
self-satisfied.

The face of the world is still today,
except for the wind
which will break
what it cannot inform.

# *Pictograph*

No sun for weeks,
under long albs of snow
saplings cracked.

A few trappers thrashed in their mats,
whiskey gone, delirious, they
dreamed a bottomless lake.

Some of us set out
assuring ourselves
the road was as far as we would get.

After we cleared the paths
the old ones called us back.
We waved our arms and smiled.

There were fans of light beyond us
in snow nobody walked before.

Blind and bitten,
we dig in silence. One boy keeps
drawing his father's face in air,
thinking of the moment
when their words ran out.

# The Gargoyles in the Garden

Inside an air-conditioned house
a man blows his trumpet.
Each day he practices,
raises the window occasionally
for relief. He sees perfection
in the hot, deserted yard, in a pool
blue and calm under the August sky.
The garden is ripe, harmony
among cosmos, zinnias, and phlox.

Someone has placed the stone heads
of two gargoyles in the garden,
their half closed eyes and gaping
mouths are triumphs of grotesquerie.

Late in the day shadows spread
across the heads of the gargoyles.
They appear to be grinning, twin voyeurs
charmed by streaked windows.
The man with the trumpet is leaving,
his dinner jacket impeccable, eyes fixed
on the face of his digital watch.

Sprinklers turn on,
night is erasing the flowers

yet the pinkish heads of the gargoyles
refuse the dark. They glisten,
though the dahlias beside them
vanish and the images of sun
in the windows and in the water have gone.
The mind of the man climbs beyond
his music, the smoke in the room,
the splash over ice, imagining
the gargoyles, their perfect No.

# In Borderlands Park

Late October woods, and in my mind
your words not to forget,
to record each image here. Everything
wants to be rendered exactly.
Afternoon sun crowns
in the blown trees, yellow
and garnet leaves swim across the air.
They never looked the same
where we come from. Gutters
backed up and on rainy Fall days
a street crew arrived with a truck
that ground up leaves, dead starlings,
junk from bus windows churned to powder.

Sidewalks echoed with the racket
of stickball, dice rattling in alleys
and crushed glass. I can't record as well
the urgent cries of chipmunks in high oaks
as I forage here, or the noise
oozing up like sighs from layers
of spongy decay.

Signs are posted: No Hunting Here.
Stumps of jack-pines, lichen paled,
crumble to peat when I tap them.
I mark these hollows for passage back
through woods where I have never walked
thinking of blind, brick alleys
as sun slices through the cracks
between tall out-croppings.
I use the light behind me
to go in deeper.
I don't need to belong to one place anymore.

In the neighborhood, you wrote, pensioners
have run out of ears for their yarns
of the Great Depression. People move in
with one year leases. The parish school
has closed and the Coolidge Theatre.
You have to have a post office box now.
There is so little left
in these woods: a thorn tree, five feet tall,
leafless, with waxy fruit dripping from its stems
becomes a crooked old woman in black, and Nonna Julia
scuttles out of the churchyard at dusk.
She is clutching her pocketbook, muttering
in Albanian. The wind rises and in the sky
a few traces of color the sun left behind.

I want to get it right, but I am not
a camera or a woodsman. I stumble
over roots not buried deep enough.
Memory filters these images
through flat layers of street amber.
The signs were posted for both of us,
wherever we are color is not light.
I have nothing more lively than words
to bring you. You already know
what is not enough.

# The Woman in the Attic

First harvest apples,
musk-warm pears, tokay grapes
and melon with grainy skin
in a basket
of woven hemp
framed for his eyes.

Outside purple finches
peck away pine scales.
Night and shadows meld.

She puts her fruit in the refrigerator,
turns the radio on. No more Danang.
Some things need cold to survive.

# Sound Prints

The wail of a siren
twists into sleep
its tail dissolves

If the siren swells
gets louder than
the dream
it may stop
her mother's keening
it had life
how could you
this is killing me

# Driving Past Clock Farm, Route 138

A New England barn faded
to slate blue, steam rising
from two young horses
in a snow field.
Nuzzling, necks sloped to strewn hay
they separate, remingle.

When I was seven,
I wanted to be with you summers
far from our brickbat street,
tending horses at Uncle Charlie's farm.
You told me moss grew greener
in the livery stable
where boards hit earth,
than anyplace outside,
how quickly it paled
after you crumbled big chunks
in your palms.

By dusk the barn is locked,
horses tight in their stalls
lulled by the hum of cars.
In each a man or woman
drives in half-light, anonymous,
leaning to the road and home.
From time to time, they bridle speed
at an intersection.

*For Joseph*

# A Day With No Name

She should be outside
tending the azaleas
but she stayed too long
at the table
watching a single spider
the clock stops ticking
letters flap in the mailbox
she won't reach for them
by noon half of her
is a lost slipper under a bed
the other half invents a cradle
pushes it into a corner
lies there listening
to a carillon
of telephone and door bells
she covers the cradle with stick figures
of druids and trombone players
she draws a water clock
a platypus a tree with blue lights
instead of leaves
when it is dark
a man with brown shoes
and a briefcase walks in
he leans down and asks
what they are having for dinner

# Seasonal

I        The harbor unlocks
           its irons of murky ice.
           Where does death's sting go?

II       Two hummingbirds slice
           through the browning pin–oak leaves,
           clean as a wind's needle.

III      Greener than new grass
           this mossy stone that names you.
           The dead are not still.

# The Redbud Opens First

I am riding a train,
night without stars
counting refractions
on sealed windows
nearing home.

Nish lived there, miscast
among lace curtains.
At sixteen he slashed his knife through
a Safeway clerk, five times,
whose carotid gushed
for thirty dollars and change.
When I get there
his mother's dark head, weight
she never again upheld,
rocked in my mother's arms.

> My hand always shakes when I try
> to draw a straight line
> from one point to another.

I had a friend who called
late at night
she couldn't breathe.
Sometimes
she took a taxi
to the Outpatient.
The resident said you don't need
Inderal, there's nothing wrong
with your heart.

She keeps reciting the litany:
a dead man's wallet beside his pillow,
a photo of a ten year old girl
where the money used to be.
His blue Buick rotting
in the driveway. Doilies wormy
beneath the Hammond Atlas.
Limoges hair-receiver crammed
with paper clips, cancelled
stamps, dead nails, gramophone,
once her head fit inside.

I never choose to recall
the dream of a woman thinning
tubers of blue iris in damp ground.
A telephone guttering through sleep
and they might as well have said
light travels at 186,000 miles per second.
It's impossible to imagine

stars are born and die
nobody knew.
Not Ptolemy, Copernicus.

      Jesus, if it passes all understanding
      how do we recognize peace?

My Aunt Mamie knew at sixteen
how to graft the branch
of a pear tree or quince,
binding each to a matrix
with a kind of poultice.
Before I wake tomorrow
a surgeon will have sliced
away her left breast.
She is eighty.
None of us ever learned
to grow life in her straight,
symmetrical fashion.

I understand we are not in heaven or hell.
We are guests of the state
the Fathers called limbo.
People in caravans circling
for centuries. Some crept
into the woods, silenced.
Others built temples for children
who sought alcoves where wind
scorched least, and the long shadows
after noon . . .

     Forgetting is a mode of action.
     Sleep, a dense text.

I follow a line
of light–eaters
who call themselves
a sorry lot of dreamers.
Fished from the runnels
of coffin ships in Boston Harbor
full of green hunger and hookworms,
they fed on visions
of the Holy Spirit rising
in the sap of New World trees.

They spun fire, air, sand,
keeping it molten
in the glassworks,
blew their breath
through long iron tubes, hoped
for perfect forms at the end.
They honed tools
to carve relief in supercooled globes,
earned day wages, mouthed public gratitude,
sure of what to expect
from this world.

In their orchards
healed branches burgeon.
The redbud opens first, then the leaves.
Memory, dance in me,
eighth sacrament, restorer.

# Gestation

*"Being an artist means, not reckoning and counting, but ripening like the tree . . ."* — *Rilke*

For years you slept
under the tree,
woke to stare at the tree
until great roots
flared up like fire
and seized you.

Through dark nights
a taproot tears
toward the barysphere.
You would be stoned
by an army of seraphim
rather than lose this ripening.

Behind your eyes
exotic birds wait to be born.
Your hair is thickening
with moss and twigs,
over your head the sky
grows itself leaf green.

Gnarled, crusty, earth-proud,
you are what you see,
learning yourself
leaf by leaf.
Your speech is the rain
riding through branches.

*For R. C.*

# Gravity

Seeds fall
force dirt
to make room
lightning splits
down a stand of pin-oak
its acorns tip
small cups
in the ground
roots curl
around water pipes
head for
the center of the earth

Rain slides
down a window
inside the room
a child probes
the fish-dark tunnel
he is
falling
for the first time
voices
name and praise
the light
he will see everything soon

Petals drop
from a blown rose

wind fills
the corners
of a ruined house
spills ancient pollen
into new graves
the empires
the children
(no one can hold them)
are falling.

# *Windfall*

In Santa Ana
unabating wind for days,
a diet of dust.
The warehouse door unlatched.
Three-thousand straw sombreros
funnel into the sky.
They are swooped up
like hollow birds.

A few flop over,
caught in a cross current.
Hot air is sucked
into their bowls,
they droop, earthbound
dry old mouths.

A woman in Magdalena
sees them fall.
She scrambles to the high plateau,
stretches her body up full.
She is dwarfed by the saguaro,
her torn apron blows over her head,
but she is shouting now,
crazy for a yellow hat.
The ribbons she forgot
for twenty years
are streaming down her back.

## Wish It Away

The winter the old man went
endless snow,
her children in and out
of the house
bringing it with them,
weeks of roads drifted
pathways blocked
and cleared again. Swags
of snow wreck the privet.

She talks
of bread rising, a lost
glove, seed for birds,
she hears herself.

Day and night
children's faces
at the window,
a northeast wind
foaming the yard,
an ocean of trees.

One summer the old man swam
to get her—
over her head,
carried her like a trophy
back through eel grass.

Later he groaned out of the mud
of nightmare, and she blocked
her ears,
the way a child must
hold fear in the dark,
reason unclear

how some can wish it away,
get moving
to Mexico City or Juneau,
solve it with sweat, an idea.
Not him.

Tough oak the wind took down
chopped to logs in May.
She counted the wide layers,
dead heartwood, his age
petrified.

# Bridge

Home from school,
she hears their voices
leaves her books in the hall,
lies on her bed, tunes out
with the Top Forty.

In the family room
her mother smokes cigarettes,
one after another, flicks
the cards fast
like they are hot.
Her partner's fingers curl tight
around each hand.

"Your deal." Annie Talbot rasps,
her mouth purple-red, cheeks
wrinkle engraved, cat scratched woman.

Her mother keeps humming
that part of an old song
about being the one and only,
the queen of hearts.

# The Subjective Case

In the middle
of the lesson
a fifth grade child
swallows the cap
of a ballpoint pen

kneel down
breathe for her
push hard
against her larynx

children run
into the hall, freeze
at the stairs
blood smudges her sweater.

At four the teacher
heads for her office
writes a report
everything she knows
the waste basket filling.

They haven't met before
the funeral home. Someone
from the family greets her:
cold hands, her throat closing,
she wanted to speak.

# After Soccer Practice

It was already dark
when I drove the boy home from the game,
but he said, "It's okay, leave me at the corner."
I knew the treeless street above the river,
that old men's eyes sprouted
from the windows at the slightest sound,
and women of all ages huddled
in winter coats near fire escapes
and sagging porches.
I guessed he would hold his breath
tight in his throat, whistle a tune
and follow his shoes over the litter
to his doorway, where the pitch of voices inside
would determine whether he went in
or walked to the river
so that the street was behind him—
and he could be confident
that the wind roughing the water
might enter and search his coat,
ask nothing of him.

# Recovery Room

They tell her again
it is only rational
to have rooms
for reawakening
and to observe rituals
such as the taking of vital signs
at ordained intervals
by men and women gowned anonymously
in sterile areas.

She does not want to return
to the chrome, enamel places.
She loathes the yes-saying faces
of dials, the click
of charts and pins, the tyranny
of children fingering her sleep.

They hammer her chest
as though it were a locked gate
to some mystical place.
They shout her name over and over.
If she speaks
she will have to repeat it
until they are satisfied.

My mother wanted her own death—
to walk into the last spiral
of her long dream,
remote as pollen braided in the hair
of any pharoah's daughter.

# What Came to Pass Among Them

Those men spoke in a dead language
passing words like closed
envelopes over cards
on the green baize
summer nights
fathers, uncles, grown-up cousins
spilling their change
under the table
half drunk at 2 a.m.

Their kids crawl out
from the bunk beds, fumble
among heavy boots
catch the falling coins
listen, go back to sleep.

The phone is ringing
her brother speaks in their tongue
what became of his dream
ten years ago
he talked straight.

Another frame breaks away
from the rotted windows
in the attic, wood sifts
to mounds beneath them.

The old men
are shut up there
in bureau drawers
in brown albums.
Cigar smoke, scrims
from a summer house
shroud them. Still with their secrets.

Someday the air will catch
a flick of ash in the sawdust.

His last stroke
her father's mouth split open
like a dead branch.
She came as close as she could
his fingers trying
to leave a message in her hand.

*For Michael S. Harper*

# Note Found Under The Eaves

'This autumn
the trees are flaming regiments.
They move in an onslaught
toward our windows, sister.

One by one, close
the blinds.     Fasten
the latches.     You must.
Such fire spreads
havoc in the marrow.

   Say: worm in the wood.
   Say: bitter at the root.

   Keep inside.

When the river has a glass body
go out and kneel beside it, dare to
rub your knuckles
into its fissures.

Stare down the thin trees
stripped of their fury,
do not believe the voices inside
that call your victory pyrrhic.
Above all, refuse
to imagine your dugs
wizened by the cold.'

# The Winter of Emily Dickinson

a long white horse
streams toward the barn's
husk    thunderheads
collapse into the field
he draws them in
leafless trees
pitch toward him

I feel
his breath    heart-race
beneath mine
we enter the snowy interior
doors close
latchstring severed.

# Natural Causes

Year after year flesh loses
its memory of summer,
her ears deafen from the sludge
of freezing quiet.

Such chill moves slowly,
the smallest details are significant:

blackbirds strip the seedbell,
they cry out from the spaces
behind winter trees,
they are hungry.
She does not move from the window.

Postal delivery leaves a package,
it sits on the porch all day.
At night a storm begins,
in her mind's eye
a rain-beaten box dissolves

and her mouth is caught
on its weighted hook,
eyes go under
countless times.

Her fingers are the last to know,
they spent lifetimes
counting and wrapping,
carding old wool
while everything they touch gets colder.
Only the faces of the dead stay warm.

## March Wind

Saturday March afternoon      wind jabs
the bricks      the ailanthus in the alley behind
Commonwealth Avenue      sun filters cautiously through
grimy windows      stairs creak      the two of them wind up
three flights where she is sleeping under the sound
of a record that turns and turns a calm Saturday
they have broken in      one hinge holds
the past level against this time      in that split second
half awake      she is screaming      over the music      out toward
the avenue and the dead bolt cracks
the police lock bends      they are in
a glint of steel arcs above her body
she does not feel beyond the first cut but hears
the rip of her jeans slashed from her thighs      thrust
of a knife      his strange sex enters her
the red edges of the knife flare through the room
blind her      smashed door tilted against the wall
shadows over them      they are leaving
her music cradled in their arms      she is rising
rocking toward the phone      halfway there she grips
a wicker rocker      on the porch back home      push and fall
push and fall back      the creaking runners echo her gasp
her mother's voice      saying time to go now      climb up
from the dark porch      safe in her bed away from the rain's
needles      sirens over wet streets      the telephone
is wet in her hands      it is her voice only      saying come
come before the dark sticky clots on her chin spill
onto the receiver      a tape spins and squawks      rewinds

at the other end     rewinds     she is lying in her first bed
a woman's voice blurring into her mother's     is slipping away
and she is telling the end of the story     two     she whispers
one taller than the other     leave your name and address
from where are you calling     she cannot say     I am
a long wound whose edges flap like wind-torn bark.

# Night People

I    I want to know how
     they find me.

II    When we visit him
     in the Ward
     my uncle says:
     'On the way to the airstrip
     a compressor roars in the truck
     I feel the dynamite, the wires,
     know what I will make
     with their joining,
     with a kick of my boot.
     Fingers lock,
     I see the red poplars
     rimming the red field.'

     He knows
     why he must live there
     and why he no longer
     does anything
     in broad daylight
     except sleep.

III    Scotch-taped to the kitchen wall
     a picture of two jonquils.
     At 3 a.m. light shines
     from the next apartment.
     Petals glow,
     sputter yellow.
     No one is watching.

IV      I wish the rain drumming
against these windows
did not resemble fingers
so I might dismiss
the image of her swollen hands,
the taxi meter
clocking the minutes
from the hospital
to our house
and back,
just once.

V      The old man rooms
above the 24-Hour Store.
He wipes his glasses,
waits for morning.
He wonders how he outlasts
the need for sleep.
Some nights he would like
to wave to the young girl below
in the red Camaro,
the Mexican
in the Buck Rogers suit.
It's all he can do
to stay put.

# December Light

Light on the windows
spackled by wet leaves, the last
of their public lives.

Out there mother and father nod
toward my room, like marionettes
soundlessly blowing their breath
through their fingers.
They kept the perennial secrets
in the tight cells
between their palms
hidden from us,
swallowed whole
like a consecrated wafer.

I can still see them
entering the vestry.
They listen for one voice
to override the wind
tell them what they wanted
to believe is true
not just the way
people did things then.

Lie down, mother, father.
You were not guilty

or innocent. Weeds
your hands impressed
ferment in compost's roil.
The past speaks to no one

of forty-seven wars on the planet,
a sun refueling itself
to rocket out of time.
The heaven you gave your days
eclipsed December light.

# How Nimble Are the Goats

At the peak of the carnival
the barker loses his breath,
the dancers, the musicians
wind down like toys.
They are caught
in a circle of light.
From their stiff embroidered coats
archers, dragons and hawks
shoot blunt arrows
past the sun's blind eye.
Nothing stirs,
there are no clocks.

The goats arrive,
they are impatient, not beautiful
but they climb
to heights
no man in this village
has tried.
Tap, go the hooves.
Jingle, go the bells.

They prance about
and butt the wooden folk.
They nibble the sleeves
of the women and force
rainbows and roses
out of their skirts.
The women's eyes darken

like moonstones, their mouths
are nailed shut, rage
stops in the feet of the men
as the goats devour their boots
and spit out the spurs like bones.

The Herder comes.
He does not enter the circle.
When he calls, the goats follow
without looking back.
And the lead dancer wakens slowly
timing his movements to the rhythm
of the Herder's vanishing cape.

Years later, the elders,
masters of forgetting, tell
only of the Herder's grace.
The young mimic the gamboling goats
in a ceremonial dance.
They wear cloven sandals
and soft fur vests.

Polishing their little horns,
the children sing of the nimble goats,
how they will devour anything,
are never afraid.
Tap, go their feet.
Jingle, go the bells.

Nancy Donegan was born in Watertown, Massachusetts and has lived in Boston and Brockton, Massachusetts, and Providence, Rhode Island. She graduated from Boston College and received an M.A. in Creative Writing from Brown University. She has received awards for writing from the Academy of American Poets and from the Massachusetts Arts Lottery Commission. She is currently teaching in the English Department at Brown University.

# POETRY FROM ALICE JAMES BOOKS